A Kid's Guide

THE
GREEN
NEW DEAL

How to Save the Planet

Practical
Green New Deal Solutions

I0087953

A FRESH LOOK AT OUR WORLD

iBooks
Manhanset House
Dering Harbor, New York 11965

bricktower@aol.com • www.ibooksinc.com

Editorial Consultant: Maartin de Kadt
Cover design by Stephen Brenninkmeyer
Cover painting by Paul Meisal
Edited by Ruth Ashby

Library of Congress Cataloging-in-Publication Data
Goodman, Billy. A kid's guide to the green new deal.
(Camelot World) "A Byron Preiss book."
p. cm.
1. JUVENILE NONFICTION / Science & Nature / Environmental Conservation & Protection. 2. JUVENILE NONFICTION / Science & Nature / Environmental Science & Ecosystems 3. JUVENILE NONFICTION / Science & Nature / Experiments & Projects, I. Title.

ISBN 978-1-59687-862-4
February 2019

A Kid's Guide To

THE
GREEN
NEW DEAL

How to Save the Planet

Practical
Green New Deal Solutions

A BYRON PREISS BOOK

by Billy Goodman
Illustrated by Paul Meisel

iBooks
Habent Sua Fata Libelli

To Becky, for keeping me well fed.
And to Alex Orzeck-Byrnes, for keeping me on
the right track.

Table of Contents

Your planet's in trouble... but it's not too late to save it. Find out what you can do to help!

Chapter 1

YOUR PLANET'S IN TROUBLE

Unless you've been asleep for, oh, say the past several years, you know that the Earth is in trouble. Turn on the TV or look at Instagram. You see pictures of garbage or dead dolphins washing onto a beach. Open a newspaper. You read that scientists predict the Earth is getting hotter. Towns all over the country are having a hard time figuring out where to stash their trash. (One garbage barge was towed thousands of miles as its owners looked for a place to dump trash from New York's Long Island) The tropical rain forests are being burned at an incredible rate. They might even disappear in our lifetime.

Environmental problems have plagued humans for a long time, but in the 1980s we recognized something new. As paleontologist Stephen Jay Gould said, "People have ruined parts of the planet before. But in the 1980s we realized we could harm the *entire* planet."

That planet, Earth, is our home. And it's the only one we've got. Astronauts may someday reach Mars or go back to the Moon. They might even establish a colony in one of those places. But humans will just be visitors—neither the Moon nor Mars has an atmosphere that people can breathe, a climate we would find comfortable, food to eat, or anything else to remind us of home.

So, we have to keep the only home we have in the best possible shape. We're going to live here a long time—we hope! It's like having an old car. You give it tender loving care; keeping it well oiled; making sure the tires are properly inflated, all the fluids and filters are fresh, all the parts are working. But the more you use the car and the more people ride in it, the harder it is to keep it running smoothly.

That's what's happening on Earth. More and more people are calling it home. So the Earth has to work harder to provide food, fresh water, and fresh air for everyone at the same time as it accepts the waste we produce.

This book will tell you how the Earth works and what you can do to help keep it working properly. You may think that you can't have much influence; after all, you're only one person and there are more than 7 *billion* other people around the world. But you won't be the only person working to save the world—if you were, the outlook would be truly hopeless. Others will be doing their part, too. Some will read this book and begin treating the planet the way they should. Other people will read other books or see television programs that will inspire them to work to save the planet. Still others may follow your example. Encourage *your* friends to learn about the environment. Convince your

parents to recycle bottles and cans. People *do* make a difference.

Ten Incredible Things You Should Know About the Earth

• Nigeria, an African country twice the size of California, had one of the fastest growing populations in the world in the 1990s. Its population was set to double in just 22 years. At that rate, the population of Nigeria would equal the entire population of the world in just 140 years.

• Twenty percent of the world's population in the rich western countries uses 70% of the world's energy.

• There are about 500 million automobiles on the planet, burning an average of two gallons of fuel a day.

Each gallon releases 20 pounds of carbon dioxide into the air.

• About 50 acres of rain forest are destroyed every minute. In one year, rain forest equal in size to the state of Virginia is lost.

• One-tenth of one percent of all the oil produced in the world each year—about 5 million *tons*—winds up in the ocean.

• By 2021, there will be just 10-15 years of landfill capacity left in the United States.

• In the 15,000 years since the glaciers pushed their way into the northern United States, the average temperature has increased nine degrees Fahrenheit. Because of the greenhouse effect, scientists fear an equal temperature increase might occur in just a few hundred years.

• If you throw away two aluminum cans, you waste more energy than one *billion* of the world's poorest people use a day.

• Would you buy something just to throw it away? About one-third of what an average American throws out is packaging.

•More than one billion trees are used to make disposable diapers every year.

Chapter 2

HOME, SWEET EARTH
The Story of Your Planet

Before you can set about saving the Earth, you need to know what you're saving. How old is the Earth? What's special about it? We need a short biography.

The Earth is about 4.6 billion years old. That amount of time is hard to imagine. How can scientists even figure out something like that? They discovered that many rocks have their own internal "clocks" that start ticking when the rocks are formed. The clocks are in the form of radioactive elements—such as uranium—that change over time into other elements. It works like this. Suppose there are ten chocolate cookies in a cookie jar. Every day one turns into a vanilla cookie. If you looked at the jar and saw six vanilla cookies, you'd know the whole jar of cookies was six days old. Similarly, if half the uranium in a rock has turned into another element, then scientists can figure out how old the rock is. This method of establishing the age of a rock is called *radioactive dating*. It is how we know that the oldest rocks found so far on Earth are nearly 4.6 billion years old.

As difficult as it is to know how *old* the Earth is, it's even harder to be sure what conditions were like at the start. Scientists agree that the early atmosphere lacked oxygen. If oxygen had been present, rocks that formed at the time would have been different chemically. Scientists believe that many gases present in the early atmosphere came from inside the Earth, escaping from volcanoes. For the first few billion years of the Earth's history, the atmosphere was probably mainly nitrogen, hydrogen, carbon dioxide, and water vapor. That mix of gases would be poisonous to any of today's animals.

The first organisms, therefore, had to be able to live without oxygen. (Some bacteria still do and are found in hot springs or at the bottom of the ocean.) Gradually, some of the organisms developed an ability to use the Sun's energy to take the carbon dioxide and water that were plentiful in the environment and make food for themselves. This process is called *photosynthesis* and is what all green plants do today. For our story this step is crucial because during photosynthesis, plants "exhale" oxygen. Gradually, the oxygen level in the atmosphere rose as more and more organisms became green plants and carried out photosynthesis. Eventually, there was enough oxygen for animals to emerge on land. Simple one-celled green plants first made the Earth a livable place for all animals, including us. As we shall see, green plants are still important today for removing carbon dioxide from the air and producing oxygen.

THE EBB AND FLOW OF LIFE

Scientists who study ancient life forms find fossils of many species—kinds—of plants and animals that no longer exist. The world has seen some amazing

HOW TO SAVE THE PLANET

species. About 300 million years ago, dragonflies with two-foot wingspans flew in primitive forests. At the same time, there were ferns as big as trees. A million years ago, mastodons roamed the North American continent. What happened to them?

They and millions of other animals and plants died out. When an entire species has disappeared, we say it is *extinct.* Judging by the fossils, many species often become extinct at almost the same time, an event called *mass extinction.* The best-known example is the

Time Line

humans evolve

dinosaurs extinct
(except birds)

first mammals

Dec. — first insects
— first fish

Nov. — first shelled organizms
— first jellyfish

Oct. — sponges

— first cells with nuclei

Sep.

Aug. — early fossils of algae-
like organisms

— stromatolites—pillars
of blue-green algae
(oxygen producers)

Jul.

Jun.

May

Apr.

Mar.

Feb.

Jan. — birth of the Earth

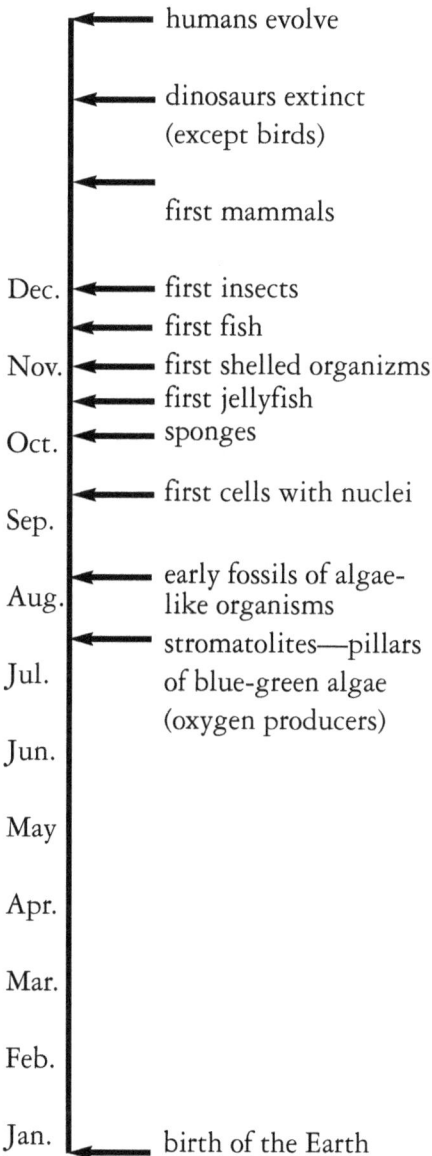

How Long Is 4.6 billion Years?

Try a little comparison. Squeeze 4.6 billion years into one year. Imagine that the Earth and the Solar System were born exactly one year ago today. By that scale, the first living things other than simple one-celled organisms appeared just a few months ago. The first fish didn't appear until about 40 days ago. The first insects came on the scene one month ago. The dinosaurs— most of them—became extinct just five days ago. The earliest humans made their appearance about six hours ago. And how long ago were you born? Less than *one-tenth of a second in the past!*

extinction of the dinosaurs. These beasts ruled the Earth for 160 million years. Yet, 65 million years ago, they and many other species became extinct suddenly (for another view of what happened to the dinosaurs, see "Are the Dinosaurs Really Extinct?" on page 13). What happened?

There are many theories to explain the demise of the dinosaurs. A large group of scientists supports a theory that one or more extraterrestrial objects— asteroids or comets— slammed into the Earth. The impacts would have started fires and thrown up enough dust and smoke to dim the Sun and cause temperatures to drop over much of the globe.

Other scientists believe that the extinctions took place more slowly, over at least 10,000 years. Some of these scientists support a theory that huge eruptions of many volcanoes over thousands of years caused the extinctions. Still other scientists point to a combination of causes that include a gradually cooling climate and increased competition for food from mammals.

Whatever the causes of the dinosaurs' extinction, it's clear that extinction is the natural end of all species. The end of a species doesn't mean that the species is a failure; it just means that the world has changed.

Unfortunately, scientists say the world is now in another period of mass extinction, and for a brand new reason. This time, people are involved. By messing up the environment—polluting the air and water, chopping down the rain forests, and draining wetlands to make way for houses and highways—people are causing species to become extinct at a frightening rate. You'll find out more about that in the last chapter.

Are the Dinosaurs Really Extinct?

I told a small fib when I wrote that the dinosaurs became extinct 65 million years ago. Most of the dinosaur species did. But scientists now believe that some lived on and have descendants that are alive today. There's no need to look for huge "terrible lizards" in the jungles of Africa. You can see these modern dinosaurs just about anywhere. They're called birds.

One of the earliest birds, *Archaeopteryx,* looked like a dinosaur with feathers.

PORTRAIT OF THE EARTH

Some facts and figures of that planet we call home:

The Earth is the fifth largest planet and the third planet from the Sun.

Circumference (at the equator): 24,901.5 miles (Boston to Los Angeles is about 2,500 miles as the crow flies; 3,017 if you drive.)

Surface area: 196,935,000 square miles (Texas is 262,000 square miles—almost a thousand times smaller.)

Percent of Earth that is ocean: 70%

Highest point: Mt. Everest, 29,028 feet above sea level

Lowest point: Dead Sea, 1,302 feet below sea level

Composition of the Earth's crust:

Oxygen, 46.6%	Silicon, 27.7 %
Aluminum, 8.1%	Iron, 5%
Calcium, 3.6%	Sodium, 2.8%
Potassium, 2.6%	Magnesium, 2.1%
Other, 1.5%	

Earth's early atmosphere

4%
water vapour

Traces of
nitrogen,
ammonia,
methane

95%
carbon dioxide

Average surface
temperature above 400°C

Earth's atmosphere today

Traces of
carbon dioxide,
water vapour,
ammonia,
methane

21%
oxygen

78%
nitrogen

Average surface
temperature 20 °C

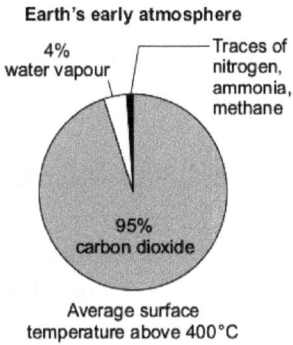

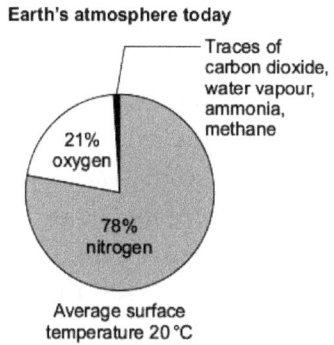

COMPOSITION OF THE ATMOSPHERE

Chapter 3

WHAT MAKES THE WORLD GO' ROUND?
How the Earth Works

Some scientists spend their entire life learning how the world works. We'll find out in one chapter. The study of how living things interact with one another and with the physical environment is called *ecology.*

The word *ecology*— coined in the 1800s— comes from the Greek word for "house."

Ecologists want to know how the inhabitants of the Big House—Earth—make their living. They want to know how one inhabitant affects another or why the population of one species sometimes explodes while the population of another species crashes. Ecologists have found that living things do only a few

different kinds of "jobs." They're either producers, consumers, or decomposers.

Producers. You know these by their more common name: green plants. Green plants are "Sun eaters." They use the Sun's energy to make their own food. Their method is called photosynthesis.

Photosynthesis is a way for plants to sunbathe and get a meal at the same time. Using energy from the Sun, plants combine water and carbon dioxide to make food. Some of the food is used by the plant right away for energy. Some is sent off to the roots for storage. And some is used to create more of the plant itself: more of the leaves, stems, and fruits that provide food for many animals.

Food isn't the only product of photosynthesis. There's also a waste product that plants don't need. It's called oxygen.

Green plants are truly a life-support system, providing food and oxygen for other living things.

Consumers. Consumers are living things that eat other living things. Some consumers eat producers. They're called *herbivores,* meaning plant eaters. When an herbivore chomps a leaf, it's eating food that was made directly with the Sun's energy. Some consumers eat other consumers. They're called *carnivores,* meaning meat eaters.

Carnivore or Herbivore?
Are the following animals carnivores or herbivores?
Grizzly bear • Chimpanzee
Human • Hedgehog

Trick question. All these animals eat both plant and animal material. They're called *omnivores.*

Decomposers. These are the vital "garbage collectors" of nature. Without them, the world would be littered with dead plants and animals. Decomposers "eat" the remains of dead plants and animals, releasing the elements that make up organisms back into the environment. Decomposers—including bacteria, fungi, and earthworms—are nature's first "recyclers."

Decomposers are found in all kinds of habitats, from deserts to rain forests to refrigerators. That's right— refrigerators. The mold growing on that loaf of bread is a fungus.

FOOD WEBS

A description of who is eating whom is called a food chain. Usually, there are many branches to the chain, so it becomes a *food web.*

Between the beginning and end of a food chain there are often many links. The chain begins with a green plant. The plant is eaten by an herbivore, perhaps a leaf-eating beetle. The beetle then walks into a trap and becomes a spider's supper. The spider is gobbled by a small bird. Then that bird is caught by a cat. When the cat dies, its nutrients are released back to the soil by decomposers and may wind up as part of another plant.

The food chain can be thought of as a path for energy. The source for all the energy passing through a food chain is the Sun.

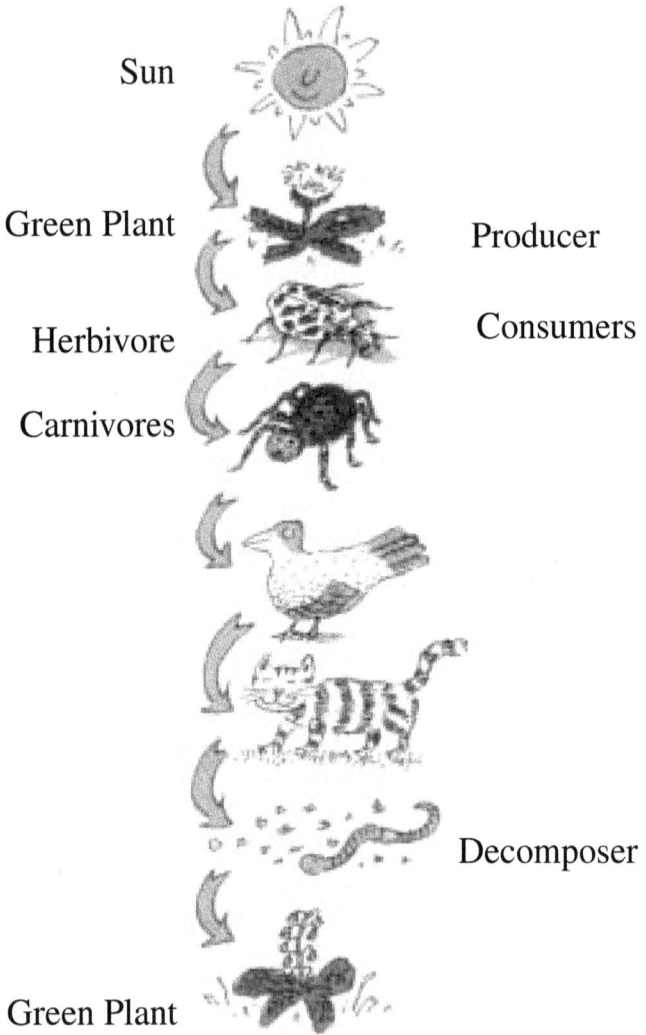

Sun		
Green Plant		Producer
Herbivore		Consumers
Carnivores		
		Decomposer
Green Plant		

FOOD CHAIN

Make Your Own Food Web

Usually, a food web refers to a particular *ecosystem,* or physical place with the animals and plants that live there. A pond is an ecosystem. So is a prairie or a field of corn. To diagram the food web for an ecosystem, you need to know what eats what.

Choose an ecosystem, or part of one, near your home and try to figure out the pattern of eating and being eaten. For example, you might take a walk in the woods and write down what you observe. What are the birds eating? Can you figure out what the squirrels, field mice, or salamanders are eating? In spring and summer, look closely at the leaves of trees or shrubs. Plant-eating insects will probably be common. With patience, you'll find predatory insects eating the plant eaters. What eats the predatory insects?

Using your observations and information from books or teachers, diagram the food web. Start with the producers near the bottom of a page and draw arrows from the plants to the herbivores and then from the herbivores to the carnivores.

You're part of a food web too, and you might try drawing that. Start with yourself at the top of the page—you're the top omnivore. Diagram the plant and animal food you eat. For each kind of food, decide whether it is a producer or a consumer. Some foods are obvious: Celery, carrots, and lettuce are plant products, so they are producers; beef and fish are from animals, so they are consumers. Some foods, however, are combinations of several ingredients, such as beef and vegetables in a stew. Others can be disguised. For example, bread is made of flour that comes from wheat, which is a producer.

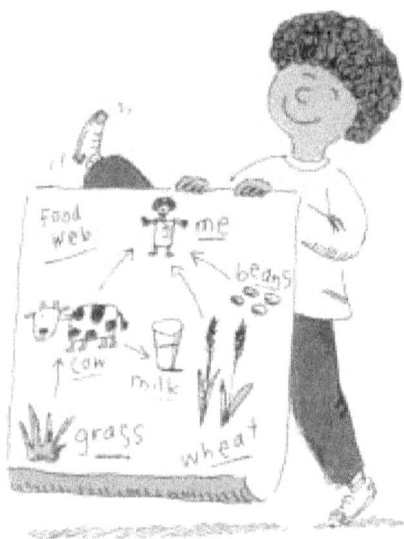

NATURE'S RECYCLING SYSTEM

Energy isn't the only thing to flow through a food chain. Atoms—the building blocks of matter—also move from one level to another.

Take carbon. Every time we breathe out, we exhale carbon as part of carbon dioxide. Some of the carbon dioxide may be absorbed by the ocean, where it can remain a long time. Some of the carbon dioxide may be "breathed in" by a green plant and made into food. The carbon in the plant's leaves, exhaled long ago by some person, may once again become part of an animal's body when the plant is eaten by a deer or any other animal.

Sometimes, nature's recycling system can take a long time and follow an odd route. For example, many plants aren't eaten by herbivores but die in a swamp and are buried in muck. The carbon atoms in the plants are trapped. Over thousands and even millions of years, given the right conditions, the plants might turn to coal. If someone discovers that coal, it can be mined and burned for energy. Then the carbon will be freed, as carbon dioxide, ready to be breathed in by another plant.

YOU SCRATCH MY BACK, I'LL SCRATCH YOURS

Some interactions between animals, or between animals and plants, are simple. Wolves in a pack are predators; their prey may be a moose that could feed them for a week. The moose browsing on plants near a pond is an herbivore and the plants are its "prey."

Sometimes, though, the interactions are more complicated. Have you seen bumblebees visiting flowers? They're gathering food, but they're not eating the flowers. In fact, visits by bees *help* flowers—or, more specifically, the plants they're attached to. Flowers reward bees for visiting by providing nectar to drink. While a bee drinks, its hairy body is dusted with pollen, the male sex cells of a plant. When that bee visits another flower, some of the pollen rubs off on the new flower. This is the way many plants reproduce. Since they can't move, they depend on bees and other *pollinators* to move for them.

If you saw one fish in another fish's mouth, you'd think the bigger fish was eating the smaller fish. But if the smaller fish is a wrasse, it's actually "vacuum cleaning" the bigger fish's mouth! Both fish benefit. The wrasse gets a meal by picking food out of

the teeth or sides of the other fish's mouth. The big fish gets its teeth brushed and mouth cleaned, helping to keep it healthy.

A CAUTIONARY TALE

Here is a story that shows how something that harms one species can harm others as well.

In many parts of the United States, and indeed the world, frogs and toads are becoming less and less common. The once-loud chirping and croaking of huge numbers of these animals is getting quieter, as their numbers decline. Why?

Scientists don't have an answer. It probably has something to do with the destruction of frogs' habitats. Some scientists have suggested that acid rain—rain that's more acidic than normal because of air pollution—might be the culprit. Many frogs and toads are easily harmed by acidity in water where they lay their eggs. The decline may have nothing to do with humans.

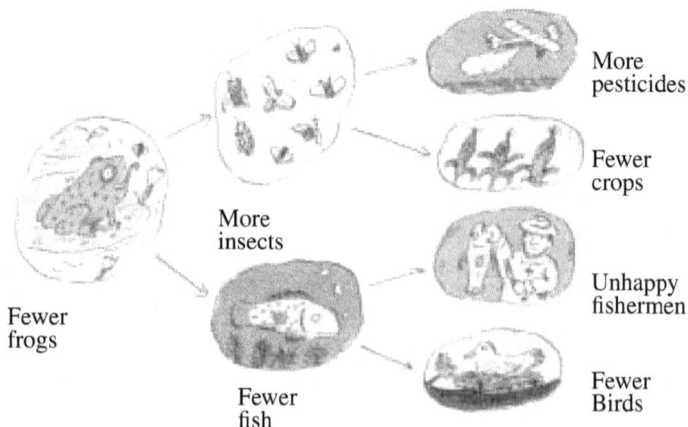

More pesticides

Fewer crops

More insects

Fewer frogs

Unhappy fishermen

Fewer fish

Fewer Birds

Whatever the reason, a decline in frog and toad populations could have far-reaching effects. Since frogs and toads normally eat lots of insects, fewer of the amphibians could lead to an insect population explosion. The larger number of insects will devour more plant food—including crops—than usual. In response, farmers may increase their use of pesticides.

Many fish eat tadpoles. So if there are fewer tadpoles, there will be less food for some fish. So fish populations might decline. That would be bad news for fish-eating birds or for people who like to fish.

The moral of this story is "You can't do just one thing." Something that affects one species is bound to affect others up and down the food chain. Can you think of other examples of this law?

Chapter 4

GROWING PAINS
Populations, Big and Small

Is the population where you live large or small? How can you tell? Is this a trick question?

Yes, because you need to know what population I'm talking about. For example, let's say I said the population in a few acres of Brazilian rain forest was 1,000,000 (1 million). If I were talking about people, then you'd guess I was kidding. The human population is too huge to fit on a few acres. But if I were talking about ants, you might guess that I hadn't counted some ants and the population was really larger. What's the difference?

Some species just take up more room than others do. People are a lot larger than ants are. A second reason is that some species use more resources than others do. One person needs a lot more food than one ant does. And one person produces a lot more waste than one ant does.

Populations that are the wrong size for their environments are often the result, or the cause, of environmental problems.

TOO FEW

The California condor is an enormous bird. Adults may weigh more than 20 pounds and have a nine-foot wingspan. As the 1990s began, the world's entire population of these majestic beasts numbered 32 birds. They live in two California zoos.

The condor was probably never a very common animal, for the following reasons:

- Its food—carrion, or dead animals—is not concentrated in one place, so the condor had to range far to find enough to eat.

- Its nest sites—places that are hard for predators to reach, such as cliffs—are spread out.

- Condors are slow breeders. In the wild, a pair has only one chick every two to three years.

What caused the condor decline? People did, in many ways. Some condors were shot. Some died from eating poisoned carrion (to kill predators, ranchers sometimes leave out poisoned bait).

Probably the main reason that the condor is in danger of becoming extinct is that it is losing its habitat to people. In central California, roads have been laid down, homes and shopping malls built, power lines erected, and farms expanded. The development squeezed out the large animals whose carcasses formed the bulk of condors' diet.

As the condor population shrank, scientists realized that the bird needed help. It was too risky to let it reproduce on its own. If just a few of the remaining pairs failed to reproduce, the species would be closer to extinction.

So the birds remaining in the wild were captured and brought to two zoos. Zookeepers helped condors breed faster than they would in the wild. When a condor laid an egg, the zookeepers removed the egg to an incubator. The bird that had laid the egg then laid a second called double clutching when she noticed the first one was gone. Now, scientists have started to release the birds in California and Arizona. It's too soon to tell, but the California condor may not become extinct. Right now it is still endangered.

TOO MANY

When Christopher Columbus reached the New World, there were 40 to 50 million deer spread out across North America. By 1900, the population had dropped dramatically, to less than a million for the white-tailed deer, the most common North American deer. First, deer were aggressively hunted. Second, towns, roads, and other development had replaced much deer habitat.

Today, deer habitat continues to shrink. But deer populations are rebounding. Part of the reason is that hunters are limited in the number they can shoot. But the major factor is probably that the deer's predators are disappearing. There are far fewer wolves and bobcats across the country than there were just 100 years ago.

The result is that a growing population of white-tailed deer, estimated at more than 15 million, is being squeezed into shrinking habitat. Deer are actually becoming a problem in many parts of the country. Here are some of the things that are happening:

• Deer can strip a small area of plants they find particularly tasty. An adult may eat ten pounds of plants a day. In some northern states, many deer starve during harsh winters because they can't find enough to eat.

• Deer must cross roads to go from one part of their habitat to another. Many are hit by cars. Collisions kill deer and damage cars.

• Deer carry the ticks whose bite can cause Lyme disease. This serious disease of humans is spreading in areas where deer populations are growing.

Think About It

Humans are the last major predator of deer. In some places deer have been shot to bring the population down and protect plants. Deer have also been captured and brought to another location. Find out if white-tailed deer are a problem in your area. If they are, what has been done about them? What do you think is the best solution? Are there some strategies that haven't been tried that should be?

HUMANS: EARTH'S MOST "SUCCESSFUL" SPECIES

In October 1999, the world population reached 6 billion. Humans may be the most successful species on Earth (although we're not the most numerous; many species of small animals, including ants, termites, and krill undoubtedly have larger populations). Humans have adapted to live in nearly every kind of habitat on the planet. And our actions control the lives of most of the other living things on the planet.

When the human population was still small, groups of people used the natural resources—food and wood, among other things—found nearby. Today, in rich countries such as the United States, we use resources from all over the world. In fact, the United States, which has just 5% of the world's population, uses 20% of the world's energy.

Most of the world's people live in poorer countries where they must still depend on resources found nearby. Their food comes from what they or their neighbors can grow or gather. They can't afford gasoline or heating oil, so they collect wood from the forests for fuel.

Humans can live in many habitats.

Human population growth is greatest in the poorer countries, for several reasons. Family planning assistance and birth control are often hard to find. And parents may want many children to help support the family. But poor countries can least afford to support more people. To feed more people, more land is plowed for crops. Some of that land, such as rain forests, is home to many plant and animal species. Some of the newly plowed land is also not very good farm land. Crops will grow for only a few years, then the land is abandoned.

No species' population can keep on increasing forever. Some populations are kept in check by predators. Some are kept down by the weather; for example, insect populations are generally smaller in areas that have colder winters. Some

populations are limited by nesting sites; for example, gray bats require two different kinds of caves during the year. There can be only as many gray bats as fill the caves.

The human population is still increasing. The Earth can support more people than it now does. But not many more.

Chapter 5

HOT AND DIRTY
Energy and Climate

The newest, and maybe the worst, environmental threat is invisible. It's not a poison. It's not radioactive. In fact, it's as ordinary as the weather. It hardly sounds dangerous. Maybe it even sounds like fun. Here's the problem: Over the next century the Earth will grow warmer. Scientists think the average global temperature will increase 2 to 6°F over the next century.

Awwright! Let's head for the beach!

Not so fast. Even a small change in the average temperature could cause major problems. We're not talking about just a change in the weather—the day-to-day temperature, winds, and precipitation. We're talking about a change in the climate—the average weather over a large area over many years.

If it's eight degrees warmer than average on a summer day, you drink more water, spend more time in the shade or in an air-conditioned building, or maybe go to the beach.

When a whole week or a whole season has unusually warm or cold weather, people talk about it. Newspapers and television feature the unusual weather in their lead stories. The warmest years of the 20th century happened in the 1980s and 1990s. Some of those warm summers also had less-than normal amounts of rainfall, resulting in droughts in the farming regions of this country. Farmers lost money, or even their farms. Electric companies had a hard time meeting the demand for energy, especially in hot cities where many people used air conditioners during the hottest days.

Summers like the ones we had at the end of the 20th century could become normal in the 21st century, scientists believe. What do they think will cause this climate change? The greenhouse effect.

THE GREENHOUSE EFFECT

It's a hot, sunny summer day. Your family's car has been sitting in a parking lot for several hours. The windows are closed, and there's no shade in sight. Are you eager to get inside?

Probably not, because the car is a small example of the greenhouse effect. It will be super-hot. The Sun's rays pass through the glass and warm the inside of the car. (The Sun also bakes the metal surfaces of the car.) The heat doesn't escape very easily from the closed interior. The glass, for example, is much less transparent to heat than it is to light.

A greenhouse for plants works about the same way. That's how the name *greenhouse effect* was given to a property of the Earth's atmosphere. Light rays from the Sun pass through the atmosphere and strike the ground. This energy from the Sun warms up the ground. The warm Earth then radiates that heat

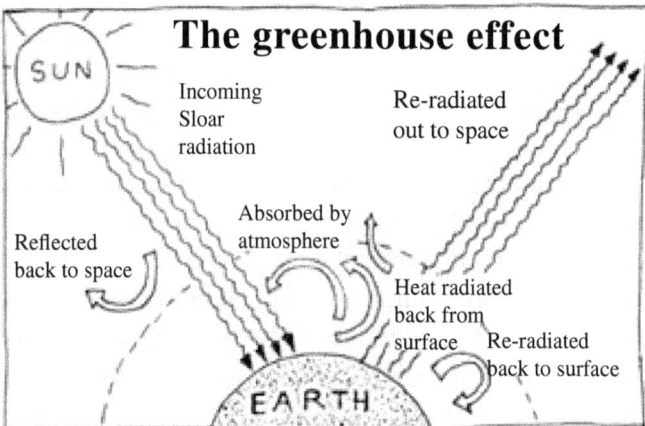

The greenhouse effect

Incoming Sloar radiation

Re-radiated out to space

Reflected back to space

Absorbed by atmosphere

Heat radiated back from surface

Re-radiated back to surface

SUN

EARTH

back toward space (you've seen that happen when waves of heat rise from a hot blacktop).

But the heat doesn't escape to space. Why not? There's no glass enclosing the Earth, but there are many invisible gases in the Earth's atmosphere that behave a bit like greenhouse glass. Water vapor and carbon dioxide are two such gases. They allow sunlight to pass through, but they trap heat and prevent it from escaping to space.

It's a good thing for life on Earth that there is a greenhouse effect. Without it, the Earth would be about 60 degrees colder on average.

So, a little greenhouse effect is good for life on Earth. But as more and more heat-trapping gases are added to the atmosphere, the greenhouse effect gets stronger. The Earth could

warm up several degrees by the middle of this century. What might some of the effects be?

• Higher sea level. As the temperature rises, the polar ice caps will melt. The sea level could rise several feet. Low-lying areas, such as southern Florida or Louisiana, would be flooded. The entire country of Bangladesh might be flooded.

• Habitats on the move. An area that has a favorable climate for certain plants and animals is called a climate zone.

Scientists have predicted that climate zones may move hundreds of miles with a change in temperature of just few degrees. Some plants and animals won't be able to keep up, and may become extinct.

• Drier, as well as hotter, weather in many places. For example, the Great Plains of the United States—the great farming region of our country—might become drier and less productive.

The causes of the greenhouse effect, as we have seen, are gases that trap heat next to the Earth. Where are these gases coming from? Some, such as carbon dioxide, are natural parts of the atmosphere. The problem is that the concentration of many gases is increasing in the atmosphere as a result of human activities. Take carbon dioxide, for example. Automobile engines release it as a waste product of burning gasoline. So do electric generating plants powered by coal, oil, or natural gas. And carbon dioxide also escapes when tropical forests are cut and burned.

ACID RAIN

Air pollution used to be something you could see. In the 1930s and 1940s, the smoke from steel-making factories around Pittsburgh, Pennsylvania was sometimes so heavy that drivers had to turn on their headlights in the middle of the day. In some cities, a smoky brown haze is still a sign that the air is unhealthy. But the greenhouse effect is one example of today's "invisible" air pollution problems.

Acid rain, a problem in some parts of the world but not others, is another. You can't tell just by standing in the rain if it's acidic enough to be harmful (even very acidic rain isn't strong enough to burn on contact, as some acids are).

Rainfall is normally slightly acidic. It might have a pH of 6, compared to a neutral solution, which has pH of 7. A liquid with a pH of 1 is a strong acid and must be handled with care. Some rain has a pH of 3 or 4, which will corrode buildings and statues over time.

What causes acid rain? When power plants burn coal or oil, they give off other gases besides carbon dioxide. One is called sulfur dioxide. In the atmosphere, sulfur dioxide can react with water vapor or other compounds to form sulfuric acid. Automobiles spew different kinds of gases called nitrogen oxides. These react in the atmosphere to form nitric acid.

The environmental effects of acid rain are sometimes hard to see. At first glance, a lake in the Adirondack Mountains of northern New York looks clear and beautiful. But if you look closer, you'll see that it's too clear. Where are the fish? Where are the plants? Where are the frogs? The lake's water has been made acidic by the steady rain of acids from above. The acidity of the water affects different species in different ways. At a pH of 6, which is only slightly acidic, some fish, such as lake trout and smallmouth bass, have trouble reproducing. Some clams and snails can't survive at all. At a pH of 5 most crayfish are dead. The lake won't have any brook trout, walleyed pike, or bullfrogs. Not all animals are harmed by acid rain. Some insects, such as water striders, do better when the lake is more acidic. But it's not because the water is better for them. Rather, it's because the fish that normally eat them are dead.

Check It Out: Acid Rain

Not every place in the United States receives acid rain. Is it a problem in your part of the country? How would you find out? You might start by asking your parents or looking in your local newspaper. Your science teacher could help, as could the

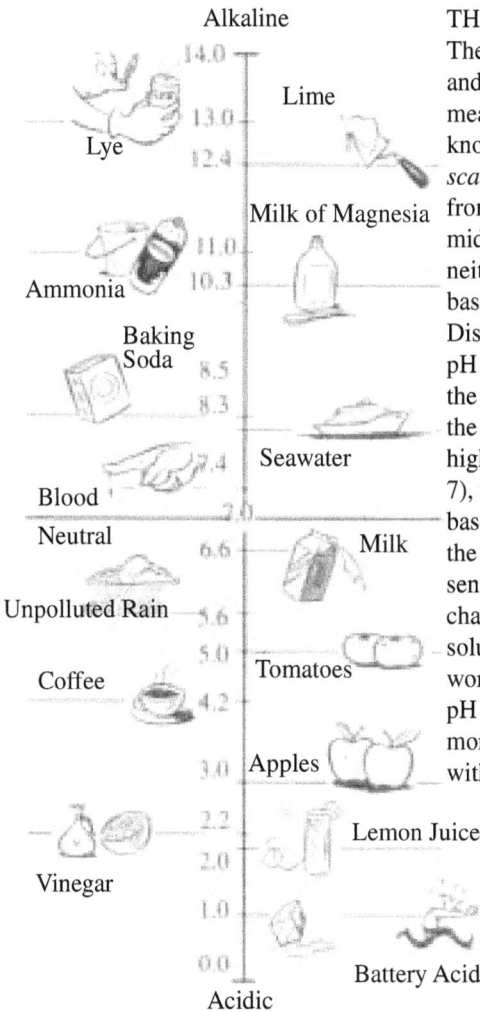

THE pH SCALE

The strength of acids and bases is measured on a scale known as the *pH scale*. The scale runs from 0 to 14. The midpoint, 7, is neither acidic nor basic, but neutral. Distilled water has a pH of 7. The lower the pH, the stronger the acid; and the higher the pH (above 7), the stronger the base. One unit on the pH scale represents a ten-fold change in the solution. In other words, a liquid with a pH of 3 is ten times more acidic than one with a pH of 4.

Alkaline

14.0

Lime

13.0

Lye

12.4

Milk of Magnesia

11.0

10.3

Ammonia

Baking Soda

8.5

8.3

Seawater

7.4

Blood

Neutral

6.6

Milk

Unpolluted Rain

5.6

5.0

Coffee

Tomatoes

4.2

3.0

Apples

2.2

Lemon Juice

2.0

Vinegar

1.0

0.0

Battery Acid

Acidic

company that supplies your electricity. Sometimes, the places that have many factories producing pollutants that cause acid rain don't suffer from acid rain themselves. This happens when pollutants are injected high into the atmosphere from tall smokestacks; by the time the pollutants have undergone the chemical reactions responsible for acid rain, they have drifted downwind. What clues would you look for to see if where you live is harmed by acid rain?

ENERGY: USE AND ABUSE

Acid rain and global warming are both symptoms of the same disease, which might be called "energy addiction." The United States suffers from this disease more than any other country does. On average, a person in the United States uses two times more energy than a person in West Germany does, two times more than a person in Japan does, and about 50 times more than a person in India does.

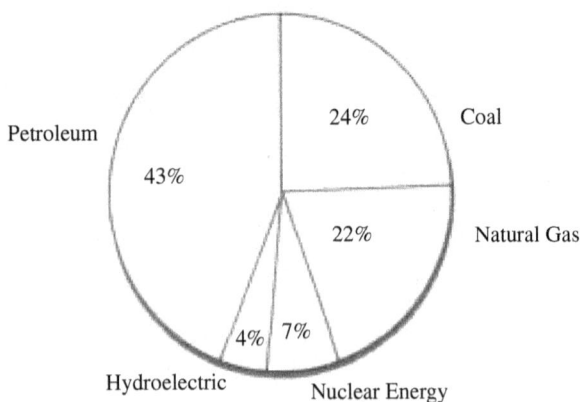

Petroleum 43%

Coal 24%

Natural Gas 22%

Nuclear Energy 7%

Hydroelectric 4%

Sources of energy in the U.S.

Where do we get our energy? A lot comes from oil, coal, and natural gas. These fuels are formed from fossils, the remains of things that were once living, so they are called fossil fuels. Leaves and stems of plants may sink in a swamp and, as years pass, more and more material is piled on top. Over the course of millions of years, the plant material is buried under tons of rock and soil deep in the Earth. The great heat and high pressure "cook" that plant material until it turns into a fossil fuel. The energy in any fossil fuel originally came from the Sun when the live plants carried out photosynthesis. When we burn a fossil fuel, we're tapping that energy.

Another source of energy is falling water. Have you ever tried to walk across a fast flowing stream? If so, you know how much energy is contained in that flow. By putting a dam across a river, engineers can convert the energy in the rushing water to electricity.

Nuclear power provides another source of energy, one not directly connected to the Sun. As the name suggests, nuclear power comes from the forces that hold together the nuclei of atoms. When the nucleus of an element is split, it releases energy. That energy is used to boil water. The steam produced this way can be used to make electricity.

Nuclear power is very controversial. One of its good points is that it won't run out like coal or oil or produce a lot of air pollution. But, of course, nuclear power has its drawbacks, too. The main one is that it produces highly radioactive waste material. The waste will give off dangerous radiation for thousands of years. No one has yet found a good way to get rid of this waste or to store it until it is no longer radioactive.

There have been some wild ideas. Some people have proposed shooting the nuclear waste into space, far from Earth. Some have suggested covering it in cement and dropping it into the deepest part of the ocean. The U.S. government is trying to come up with a plan for waste produced in this country. For years, the U.S. government has tried to come up with a plan for waste produced in this country. They have shipped it to parts of the country where few people live, and they have paid poorer nations to accept it. But these plans affect the people and animals that live on the land where the waste is dumped.

ENERGY CONSERVATION

Usually when people flick on a light switch or fill up a car with gasoline, they don't think about the energy supply running out. But in 1973, the United States got a shock when a group of oil-producing countries briefly stopped selling oil to this country. Suddenly, gasoline and other petroleum-based products were in short supply. People waited in line at gas stations for hours to fill their cars.

Since that time, we've realized that we have to conserve energy. That means making the supplies we have last longer by using less. Fossil fuels such as oil and coal are called nonrenewable resources. Someday, the plants and animals that are buried in swamps now may become fossil fuels. But that someday is so far in the future that when we use up the current supply of fuel, there'll be nothing to replace it.

What You Can Do

By using less energy, you and your family will be doing your part to protect the Earth's climate, since energy use releases carbon dioxide. You'll also help to reduce acid rain and other forms of air pollution and to conserve fuel. Look around your home for places where you may be wasting energy. Here are some common places for improvement:

• **Turn off lights.** The typical light bulb ought to be called a "heat" bulb, because heat is what it makes best. About 90% of the energy used in lighting a standard bulb (called "incandescent") is lost as heat. So, turn off lights when you leave a room. And use fluorescent lights where you can—they use much less energy.

• **Turn off other electric gadgets when not in use.** Televisions, stereos, and radios don't use a lot of energy, but why waste any?

• **Don't do electrically what you can do by hand.** Open cans by hand. Sharpen pencils by hand. Take the stairs rather than the elevator.

• **In the summer, use fans instead of air conditioners.** Fans use only one-tenth the energy of an air conditioner. Therefore, they produce only one-tenth the pollutants.

• **In the winter, turn your thermostat down five degrees and wear an extra sweater.** This will cut your heating bill by as much as ten percent. Also, you'll be using less energy and putting fewer air pollutants into the air.

• **Plug leaky homes.** Heating and air-conditioning account for about half the energy used at home. In many homes, lots of heat leaks out through cracks around windows and doors. Do you know how much oil it takes to heat the air that escapes from all the homes in the United States during a year? *Half the output of the Alaskan pipeline!* (The pipeline carries oil from wells on the north coast of Alaska across the state to the port of Valdez.) Check for drafts around windows or doors. Look for

moisture on the insides of windows on cold days. That means the windows aren't doing a good enough job keeping heat in.

• **Use less hot water.** Does that mean taking cold showers? Not at all. Just be smart. Don't keep the hot water running in the sink. When washing clothes by machine, rinse in cold water.

• **Encourage your family to drive less.** Cars and pickup trucks are responsible for about 20% of the carbon dioxide released into the air. So, whenever possible, walk, bike, or take a bus or the subway.

Chapter 6

FOOD, GLORIOUS FOOD
Feeding the Human Family

Imagine what the world would be like without agriculture. No more corn on the cob. No bread. No hamburger. Getting a meal wouldn't be as easy as walking into a fast-food restaurant. Some of us would have to collect wild plant foods such as seeds, nuts, and berries. Others would fish or hunt.

That's what our ancestors had to do. They were called hunter-gatherers. Before agriculture was invented, all people were hunter-gatherers. These people lived in small family groups. Almost everyone was involved in getting food for the group—and it took all day. Because each group had to feed itself with whatever game it could kill or plant food it could collect, group size was necessarily small. Even so, the group might have to migrate occasionally as game animals moved or as the gatherers collected all the fruits and nuts growing in an area.

So there were no cities before agriculture was invented. The entire population of the world was small and spread out.

Everything changed about 10,000 years ago, anthropologists believe. Agriculture probably began first in the Near East, a region called the Fertile Crescent that today includes Lebanon, Israel, Syria, Jordan, Iraq, and Iran. Agriculture was born separately at about the same time in Central America and in eastern Asia.

What is agriculture, anyway? It is the growing of crop plants and the raising of animals for the specific purpose of feeding people. There are no written records to tell us how agriculture began, but people have guessed. Animals may have been domesticated this way:

For a long time, hunters killed whatever animals they could find and capture. They learned how certain animals behaved, so they knew the best way to hunt them. They began following herds of animals that migrated with the seasons. It may have occurred to some innovative hunter-gatherer (or several) that they could capture young animals and raise them. At this point, people became shepherds.

Plants were probably domesticated when people realized, perhaps by accident, that if they stuck some seeds in the ground, plants would grow. Instead of depending on wild wheat, they could plant seeds where they wanted the wheat to grow.

Food Where You Live

A few hunter-gatherer tribes still survive, in remote regions of the tropics. What if you suddenly had to become a hunter-gatherer? What foods could you find in the environment around you? Don't count cultivated crops or domestic animals; try to list only wild foods. Some examples to get you started: acorns, pigeons, sunfish.

MODERN AGRICULTURE

However it happened, agriculture led to the human population explosion. People settled in one place. A few people could produce enough food for many others. Whereas before people hadn't remained in one place long enough to pollute it, now they began to have an effect on their environment.

There may have been 5 million people in the entire world 10,000 years ago. By 2,000 years ago, the number had

reached about 200 million. It's now more than 6 billion, and it could reach 9 billion by 2050.

To produce food for so many people, farmers and ranchers around the world must overcome many obstacles. They

Growth of Human Population

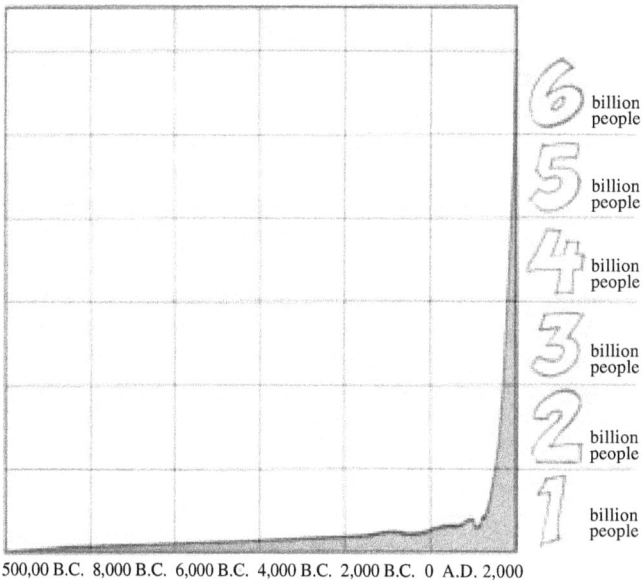

6 billion people

5 billion people

4 billion people

3 billion people

2 billion people

1 billion people

500,00 B.C. 8,000 B.C. 6,000 B.C. 4,000 B.C. 2,000 B.C. 0 A.D. 2,000

face bad weather—drought, too much rain, early frosts. They face pests—insects and weeds—and disease. They face the loss of soil and its fertility. They face economic problems.

In overcoming these obstacles, agriculture creates environmental problems of its own. Here is a description of some of them:

Water pollution. When you think of water pollution, you probably think of a pipe dumping dangerous chemicals directly into a stream or lake. That's pollution from a specific source. But agriculture is a *nonpoint source* of water pollution, meaning that the pollution doesn't come from one point. When crops are watered, by rain or irrigation, only some of the water is absorbed by the plants. Some evaporates. The rest has just two places to go: It can run along the surface until it reaches a lake, a stream, or the ocean. Or it can trickle down into the ground until it reaches an underground stream known as *groundwater.*

Water doesn't travel alone. It carries with it lots of soil. It carries fertilizer, insecticides, herbicides, and fungicides. This "baggage" makes water poorer for drinking and poorer as a habitat for plants and animals.

Where Does Your Drinking Water Come From?

Drinking water has two sources. It can come from surface water, such as reservoirs or rivers. Or it can come from groundwater, in which case it must be pumped to the surface by a well. Where does your water come from?

Erosion. It's hard to think of soil as a natural resource; isn't it just dirt? But, in fact, the loss of soil— *erosion*—is a serious environmental problem in many parts of the world, including the United States. Water carries soil away and wind blows it away.

The upper layer of soil—called *topsoil*— contains organic matter and is usually very fertile. It takes nature hundreds of years to build several inches of topsoil. Erosion can remove it quickly.

What leads to erosion? Exposed soil erodes more quickly than does soil covered by vegetation. The soil on a hillside erodes more quickly than does soil on a plain. Many farmers no longer leave fields bare if they are not growing a crop on them. Instead, they plant grass to help hold the soil in place.

Desertification. This word means "making a desert." How, you ask, can people make deserts? Aren't deserts just the result of a hot, dry climate? Climate *is* important, but people can help turn a dry grassland into a desert. One place where a new desert is being born is in the Sahel, a region of Africa just south of the Sahara Desert.

Many people in the area have traditionally tended herds of animals. The shepherds and their animals moved from one place to another, following the rains just as wild herds do. In this way, the shepherds let the land "rest" and recover.

For a variety of reasons, some political, people began to settle in towns and villages. Governments dug wells, so that there would be water available year-round. Now the land never gets a rest. Near the well, cattle eat the vegetation and trample it. Gradually, the vegetation is being destroyed and the underlying soil eroded. What is left is a desert.

Desertification is not just a problem of arid countries in Africa. It happens in the United States too, especial y where cat le graze on dry grasslands. When a few dry years hit the Midwest in the 1930s, much soil blew away, creating what is known as the Dust Bowl.

Pesticides. If you could travel back in time to the Great Plains 500 years ago, you would find it covered by large prairies— grasslands with many kinds of grasses, some shrubs, and few trees. Many animals inhabited the region: bison, coyotes, jackrabbits, prairie dogs, black-footed ferrets, field mice, snakes, hawks and other birds, and loads of insects.

Today, in the same area, instead of a prairie you're likely to come upon acres of corn or wheat. Stretching as far as the eye can see, there will be just one kind of plant. Most of the animals will be gone, too.

But there'll be some animals the farmer doesn't want: insects that eat the crop or weeds that compete with the crop for nutrients. These are called pests. A huge cornfield is as attractive to an insect as a freezer full of ice cream is to you. Food and nothing but food.

To protect their crops, most farmers resort to pesticides, poisons that kill the pests. Insecticides, for example, kill pest insects. But they also kill *beneficial* insects, which help farmers.

Some beneficial insects are predators or parasites that eat pest insects. Often, beneficial insects help keep the pest population small. If the predators are killed by insecticides, they'll not be able to keep the pest population in check. Usually, the pest population recovers faster than the slower breeding predators do. Therefore, an odd result of some pesticide spraying is that pests get worse!

Other beneficial insects pollinate crop plants. Many crops require pollinators, such as honeybees, in order to produce fruit or grain. If insecticides kill the pollinators, the crop may suffer.

Pesticides may also harm other wildlife and people, especially if used improperly. Workers have to be careful not to breathe in pesticides or get them on their skin. Pesticides can accidently harm wildlife, either by directly poisoning them or by working their way up the food chain.

BIOLOGICAL CONTROL

As long as there have been green plants, there have been insects that eat them. In most cases, herbivorous insects don't kill the plants they eat. Other insects—predators and parasites—keep the herbivores in check. Many farmers hope to take advantage of nature's own *biological control.*

To use biological control, farmers release beneficial insects into their fields. They have to know what pests are attacking their crops, then find the proper helpful insect. When using biological control, farmers don't spray insecticides, because the poisons will also kill the beneficial insects.

Often, insect pests have come to the United States from another country. Harmful aphids, mites, or beetles might stow away on shipments of products or they might even be caught on the wheels of an airplane. The pest might have been kept in check back in its home country by a predator. In a new country, without the predator to keep its population small, the pest's population explodes.

That's exactly what happened in the case of the Russian wheat aphid. This tiny insect lives on the leaves and stems of wheat and other grasses. It sucks juice from the plants and makes them sick. The aphid comes from the Caucasus region and Central Asia. Somehow, it got to Mexico around 1980; scientists suspect it stowed away on airplanes. A few years later, the aphid flew across the border and landed in Texas. Now, it is found in all western states.

As the name suggests, the Russian wheat aphid is a pest of wheat. By reducing yields, it has cost farmers a lot of money. Scientists are trying to find natural enemies of the Russian wheat aphid. They have traveled to Russia and other countries to find beetles and wasps that will eat the aphid. They bring these enemies back to the United States and release them into wheat fields. It will take a few years for the populations of the enemies to grow enough for them to keep the aphid under control.

TROPICAL RAIN FORESTS

Tropical rain forests are the steamy jungles shown in movies, where it's always hot and it rains every day. They are home to more than half the world's plant and animal species. If you were to go to a woods near your home and count the different kinds of trees you find in a few acres, you'd be lucky to find 30. In many parts of the tropical rain forest, a few acres are home to *more than 200 species* of trees.

And, of course, the forests are full of other life: monkeys, jaguars, toucans, capybaras (the world's largest rodent), tapirs, and piranhas. And insects of all descriptions: army ants and leaf-cutter ants; cockroaches; katydids; termites; butterflies and moths; bees and wasps.

This biological preserve is in trouble. Fifty acres of rain forest disappear worldwide *every minute.* People move into rain forests in the hopes of scratching out a living on the land. In Central America, cleared forests become pasture for beef cattle. Who eats the beef? It's mostly for export to the United States and other developed countries where it winds up in pet food, soup, and other products.

In Central and South America and in Asia, poor people also burn the forests in order to open up space for farming. In Africa and Asia, the forests are a major source of fuel for cooking, heating, and even industry. In fact, half the world's population relies on wood for fuel. Lest we think that the problem of forest destruction is purely a Third World problem, consider these facts:

• In a year, the average American uses as much wood in the form of paper as the average resident of the developing world burns as fuel.

• During the early history of the United States, and in Hawaii today, forests were cleared for some of the same reasons that rain forests are cleared today.

Since the rain forests are so incredibly rich, it might seem like the soils under them would be good for agriculture. That's not the case. Tropical soils have a thin topsoil. Most of the nutrients in the forest are in the vegetation. That's why agriculture in many parts of the rain forest is known as *slash and burn*. The forest is cut, left to dry, then burned. The fires leave behind ashes that are rich in nutrients that can be absorbed by crops.

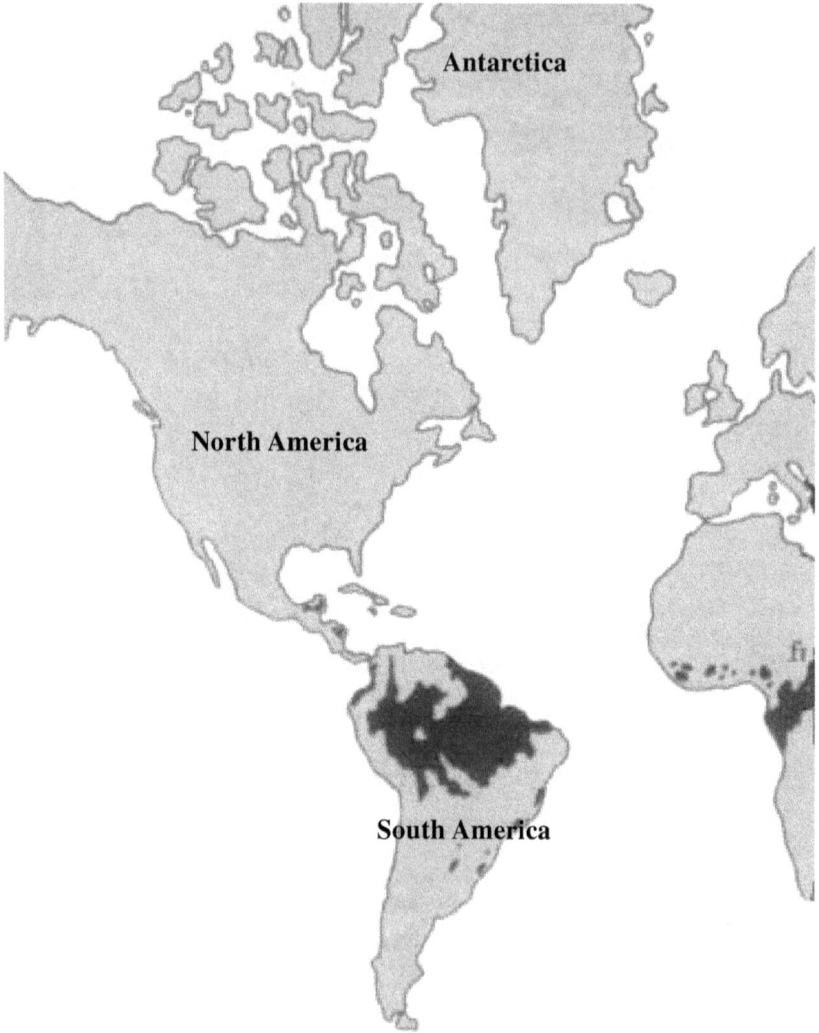

Antarctica

North America

South America

fr

RAIN FORESTS OF THE WORLD

When the forest is cleared and crops planted, there is much less protection against erosion. The heavy rains of the tropics wash away soil and nutrients.

So it turns out that the newly created farmland may only be good for a few years. Then, the farmers must move on and clear more rain forest.

KIDS WHO MAKE A DIFFERENCE:
RAIN FOREST PROTECTION

The San Francisco earthquake of 1989 did more than just interrupt the baseball World Series. It postponed World Rain Forest Week at Marina Middle School in the city. Allyson Woodman, an 8th-grader at the school, had worked with science teachers and friends to bring programs about the rain forest to her school. They were held as planned, a few weeks late. Allyson was committed to the environment and to saving the planet. "I'm interested in environmental problems," she said, "I'm not interested in hair spray." For rain forest week, she and her friends visited classes to tell them what the rain forests are, where they are, and why they're in trouble. She collected signatures on a petition that went to the Japanese government, complaining about the large amount of rain forest wood that country imports. At home, Allyson recycled, bought organic produce, and followed a vegetarian diet. "Meat clogs your arteries," she said. She hoped to keep interest in the rain forest high at her school by organizing an activist group after school. "There are people doing things about environmental problems," she said, "but not enough."

Rain Forest Products

Make a list of products that come from the rain forest. Compare your list with those of others. You might be surprised at how many everyday items come from the rain forest, including bananas, chocolate, and vanilla.

What You Can Do

The more you know about where your food comes from, the better you'll be able to make choices that protect the environment. If you can, visit a farm and find out how it works. Farmers depend on the land and have a strong reason to try to protect it. Farmers' markets in cities are also good places to meet and talk to farmers.

• **Try to buy organic fruits and vegetables if you're concerned about pesticides.** Organic produce is grown without man-made fertilizers or pesticides.

• **Don't be wasteful of forest products.** As you'll see in the next chapter, Americans throw away more paper than any other kind of trash. Try not to buy products with too much paper packaging—it'll just be thrown away. Use recycled paper whenever possible, and recycle your own newspaper and other paper. The back of used sheets of paper makes good scrap paper for notes, rough drafts, or math problems.

• **If you think a product was made at the expense of the rain forest, don't buy it and tell the seller why.** Some furniture is made with wood from rain forest trees, including mahogany and teak. Some beef products come from cattle grazed on cleared rain forest land. Fast-food restaurants say they don't use rain forest beef, but it doesn't hurt to ask and to express your opinion.

• **Favor products that can be harvested from the rain forest without cutting it.** For example, a candy called Rainforest Crunch contains Brazil nuts and cashews from the Amazon. Find out what products come from the rain forest. Learn which ones require that the forest be cut and try to avoid them.

• **Plant trees.** Not only do trees absorb carbon dioxide, but they also help shade houses and reduce the need for air conditioning.

• **Get others involved.** You might form a student group. Write to government officials to tell them what you think. Senators and representatives read their mail and are often influenced by the voices of only a few of the people they represent.

Chapter 7

WHAT A DUMP
Getting Rid of Waste

We're pros at throwing things away. An orange peel at breakfast. An empty cereal box. The plastic we wrap our sandwich in for lunch. The paper bag we bring our lunch in. Banana peels. Moldy bread we forgot about in the back of the refrigerator. The newspaper we finished reading. Plastic yogurt containers and soda pop cans.

All these things and more wind up in the trash can when we finish using them. Our trash is collected along with everyone else's trash and taken—where?

Not too long ago, everything went to the dump. This was just a big pit on the outskirts of town. Trash was simply dumped in. Nowadays, dumps are called "sanitary landfills." The main difference? Tractors push dirt over the garbage. Some sanitary landfills are made in ways that try to protect the environment. For example, they may have plastic liners at the bottom to catch any water trickling through the trash. About 80% of our trash goes to landfills. The rest is incinerated (10%) or recycled (10%).

LANDFILLS

When we bury garbage, we tend to forget all about it. But it doesn't disappear. Under the ground, with little oxygen to help bacteria eat the garbage, almost nothing happens to it. Scientists have dug into landfills and found ears of corn still intact after 20 years and newspapers still readable after 30.

Because most trash doesn't disintegrate, landfills eventually fill up. Chances are that by the time you finish high school, the landfill your community uses will be full. When that happens, towns sometimes have to truck their trash hundreds of miles at great cost, to another dump. It's rare for a new landfill to open—after all, who wants one in the backyard?

What winds up in a landfill? As the pie chart shows, pretty much anything.

What's in Our Trash?

The diagram shows what Americans throw out (by weight). It is an average of communities across the country. How do you think the trash from Austin, Minnesota (a farm town of

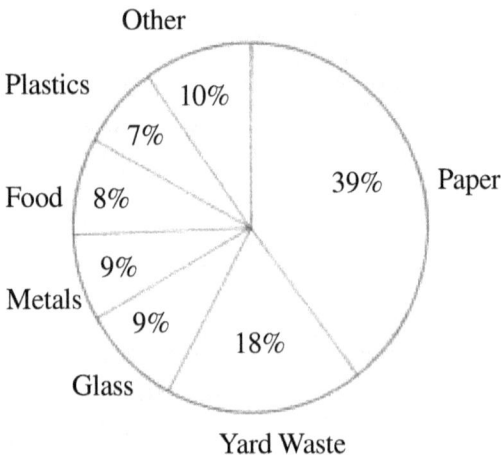

Other
Plastics
10%
7%
Food 8%
39% Paper
9%
Metals
9%
18%
Glass
Yard Waste

about 25,000), compares to the trash from St. Louis, Missouri (a city of about 500,000)?

INCINERATORS

These are places that burn trash. Trucks dump the trash in a huge building that looks like an airplane hangar. Then the enormous jaws of a crane grab a mouthful of trash and dump it onto a 2,000 degree F fire. Now that's hot!

Some incinerators do more than just burn the trash. The heat they generate boils water, and the steam is used to make electricity.

Burning would seem to be the perfect solution to the trash crisis, especially when electricity is made, too. If you've watched paper burn in a fire, you know that what's left takes up a lot less space. But incineration has a few problems.

First, when trash is burned at high temperatures, many gases are produced that go up the smokestack. Some of these gases, such as dioxin, can be harmful to people near the stack. Incinerators can be built so that almost all the harmful gases are removed from the smoke before it leaves the stack. Second, stuff that won't burn— *ash*—is left after incineration. Ash contains metals, such as lead and cadmium, that are dangerous to people and must be disposed of properly. Many scientists say the ash must be handled like other hazardous waste: put in a landfill specially made to capture any water that trickles down through the waste. The water, say from rain, can dissolve the metals and carry them lower into the ground, possibly contaminating groundwater.

How Much Trash Do You Make?

The average American makes about 3.5 pounds of trash a day. Are you and your family average? This easy project will tell you. Perhaps it will even get on the road to recycling.

The plan: Simply collect your trash using separate containers for different materials—metals, glass, plastic, paper, and food waste. Weigh the trash at the end of the experiment. The total weight collected divided by the number of days of the experiment gives the weight of trash your family tosses each day (example: 50 pounds in five days equals ten pounds a day). The weight per day divided by the number of people in your family gives the average weight each person tosses each day (example: ten pounds a day tossed by four people equals 2.5 pounds per person per day).

Some tips:

• Continue to use your main trash can with a plastic liner for food waste and food contaminated paper, such as the paper the fish for supper was wrapped in. If you normally use a garbage disposal, put the garbage in the food container for the experiment.

• Use a separate paper bag or large box for plastics, glass, metals, and paper. Rinse the glass and metals, so they don't smell.

• Continue the experiment for at least a few days, to get a true picture of your trash.

• By separating the materials in your trash, you'll see what you could be recycling.

RECYCLING

If you think of an empty soda can as trash, well of course you'll throw it away. But here's what an empty can really is: a raw material.

Making a new can from scratch uses the equivalent of half a can of gasoline. Making one from an empty can uses much less energy.

Recycling has lots of benefits and few drawbacks. With an active recycling program, much less trash will go to landfills. Our landfills will be able to stay open longer and accept the trash that *can't* be recycled. In most cases, recycling cuts the amount of energy used to make a new product.

The main drawback of recycling? It takes work! In order for a recycling program to work, you have to help out. You can sort your trash into some of the following categories, depending on how your community's program works:

• **Glass.** Some glass bottles are simply cleaned and reused. Other kinds of glass are cut up and used to make new glass.

• **Metals.** Any and all metal cans are recyclable. Don't forget aluminum foil and frozen food trays.

• **Paper.** As you saw from the diagram, paper of all kinds is the main thing we throw away. Much of it can be recycled—especially newspaper and high-quality white paper like the kind you take notes on in school.

• **Plastic.** Surprised? Many kinds of plastic can be recycled, but they must be separated from each other. One of the most commonly recycled plastics is called *polyethylene*

terephthalate (PET). You know it as the clear plastic bottles with the colored bottom used for soft drinks.

You may have heard of a kind of plastic that's supposed to fall apart after use. It's called degradable plastic. Some people believe that it might help ease the trash crisis because after weeks or months it can disintegrate. But most environmentalists think *degradable* plastic is a bad idea. It only disintegrates in strong sunlight, so it won't disintegrate in the conditions of most landfills. More importantly, degradable plastic *can't* be recycled. You're better off using plastic bags that can be recycled, or better yet, using bags you can reuse.

Look for the recycling symbol when you shop.

KIDS WHO MAKE A DIFFERENCE: CUTTING DOWN ON TRASH

Jessie Lyman said, "We thought we could do something. We really, really wanted to do something." She was only nine years old when she said this, but the Freeport, Maine, third grader and her friends proved that kids who want a better environment had better be listened to.

Jessie and her friends were upset about the hamburger containers and other disposable plastic items being used by a fast food restaurant in their coastal town. They worried that sea animals would eat discarded plastic. When the plastic is broken up into little pellets, animals think it's food. But they can't digest it. The plastic also litters the streets and doesn't break down.

So Jessie and her friends made signs saying "Ban Styrofoam" and marched with them in a parade in Freeport.

They went before the town council and asked the council to ban Styrofoam in their town. The council listened to all sides and then voted in favor of the kids. No more Styrofoam.

Jessie says other kids can make a difference. "First, just stop using stuff that might hurt the environment," she says. "Second, try to help the environment by doing what we did: banning something or supporting an environmental group."

What You Can Do

You can help solve the solid-waste crisis. The new watchwords are reuse and recycle.

• **Try to avoid products that are used once and thrown away.** Instead of a paper cup or a Styrofoam cup, why not use a glass? At cookouts, try to use washable instead of disposable plates and utensils.

• **Shop for products that have less packaging.** You can get fruit and vegetables, for instance, without plastic wrapping.

• **Encourage your local grocery store to carry both paper and plastic bags.** Carry your own string bag to the store to bring groceries home in.

• **Find out what items are recycled in your community and recycle them.**

• **Support recycling by buying recycled items.** Look for the recycling symbol on these products. You can often find greeting cards made from recycled paper.

• **Encourage your friends, your family, and your school to recycle and reuse.** You may be able to convince your community to start a recycling program or to improve the one it has.

Chapter 8

WILDLIFE ALERT
Saving Species

Life would be pretty bleak for us humans if there were no other animals or plants. In fact, life would be impossible. Think about it:

• What would we eat? Just about all our food was once alive or came from something alive.

• What would we breathe? Our oxygen comes from plants, which make it during photosynthesis.

• What would we use to treat disease?

Many medicines come from plants, animals, or microorganisms. Examples include penicillin (an antibiotic, or antibacterial drug), which comes from a mold, and a drug from the venom of a Malayan pit viper (a relative of the rattlesnake), which helps prevent blood clots from forming.

We get plenty of other benefits from plants and animals. Take forest trees, for example.

The trees themselves provide wood, for building, for furniture, and for other products. But the trees don't have to be cut down to be useful. They help to hold the soil, preventing erosion. Trees even help recharge the underground stream known as groundwater. By slowing down running water, they allow the water to sink into the soil rather than run off to the sea.

And, of course, without plants and animals, there'd be no woods to hike in, no vegetable garden to tend, no dog to play with.

THE EXTINCTION CRISIS

Unfortunately, many plants and animals are becoming extinct. As you read in Chapter 2, extinction is the natural end of all species. Biologists believe, however, that we are living in an age of mass extinction caused largely by humans.

Long ago, our ancestors probably wiped out some species. About 12,000 years ago, many species of large mammals disappeared in North America. Imagine: Roaming what we know as the Great Plains were mammoths, giant sloths, and saber-toothed tigers. There's some evidence that these species were hunted by humans who had come into North America across the Bering Strait. (At the time, land connected what are now Siberia and Alaska.)

Closer to the present are more examples of humans causing extinctions. A few hundred years ago, European sailors found a fat, flightless bird (called the dodo, from the Portuguese for "foolish") on the island of Mauritius, in the Indian Ocean. Sailors ate some and brought others back to Europe. What really

did the bird in, however, was what the sailors brought to the island: pigs, dogs, and cats. These animals roamed over the island and ate the eggs and nestlings of the dodo. The dodo was last seen in 1681.

Today, scientists estimate that at least one species of bird or mammal becomes extinct every year. Most of this extinction is going on in the rain forest, where about half of all the species in the world live.

How Many Species?

Scientists aren't sure exactly how many species of living things there are. They have given names to about 1.5 million species (including roughly 1 million insects). But there are many more that don't have names, and more still that haven't even been discovered. The best guess scientists have is that there are about 10 million species.

What are people doing that is causing so many species to become extinct or at least endangered?

Hunting. Humans are a hunting species. We have killed animals for food, for clothing, and for a variety of other products. For example, hunters will kill a rhinoceros for its horn, an elephant for its ivory tusks, or a bird for its feathers. With modern weapons and other means to capture animals, hunters can drive species toward extinction.

Collecting. You can find some exotic plants and animals in people's yards and homes. To have a pet bird or a cactus in the yard, some people will buy animals and plants that shouldn't be collected. Even some zoos have been caught buying illegally collected animals.

Every year, about 3.5 million birds are captured from the wild *legally* for the pet trade. Donald Bruning, curator of birds at the Bronx Zoo, estimates that for every bird in a pet store, as many as 100 died before they could make it to a store. Many birds are caught illegally. Some species, such as the hyacinthine macaw of Brazil, have become endangered solely from being hunted for the pet trade.

Destroying habitat. Habitat is another name for a plant or animal's home. Habitat destruction is a big problem worldwide. As the human population grows, we cut down forests to grow crops, to provide grazing space for animals, or to provide lumber to build cities. We fill in swamps. We plow prairies to plant crops. Every time we destroy natural habitat, we destroy the home of some plants and animals.

KIDS WHO MAKE A DIFFERENCE: DIET FOR DOLPHINS

Do you think that ever-popular tuna surprise on school lunch menus around the country is harmless? Not according to kids like Laura Nelson. Nelson and some classmates at Gateway High School in Aurora, Colorado, convinced the school district to boycott tuna because many dolphins used to die in fishing nets set for tuna. Schools in Milford, Connecticut, also bowed to student pressure and stopped serving tuna.

Nelson and her friends learned about the dolphin-tuna connection during a school trip to the Dolphin Research Laboratory in Grassy Key, Florida. They saw a film secretly taken on a tuna fishing boat. The scenes of the dolphin slaughter bothered the students so much that they decided to do something. They visited classes and lectured about the problem. They wrote a petition and circulated it throughout the school district. They brought the petition before the school board, which eventually agreed to stop buying tuna for the schools.

Nelson said, "It wasn't a really big sacrifice for me, but it's a statement. I've gotten relatives and some of my neighbors to stop eating tuna. Schools from outside the state have expressed interest in the tuna boycott."

Some students doubted that just a few kids could have much effect. But, said Nelson, "You take a small step it just takes one voice and pretty soon everyone else will hear about it and will do something." Many other people joined the boycott. By 1992, the tuna boycott had succeeded in its goals and was ended. Dolphin deaths in one area of the Pacific shrank from 27,000 annually to less than 2,000.

HOW CAN WE SAVE SPECIES?

It's our fault that many species are endangered, so it's our responsibility to try to slow the extinction crisis. There are a variety of tactics for saving a species, depending on how much danger it's in.

Protect Habitat. The best way to save a species if it's not too bad off in the wild is to protect its habitat. The habitat must be big enough to support a reasonably large population of the species—if you protect just enough habitat to save three elephants, sooner or later there'll be no elephants.

But if people can protect a large area of undisturbed habitat, the animals and plants within it will save themselves. By keeping wild areas undeveloped, environmentalists can protect many species at once. The entire ecosystem will remain healthy. Imagine you're trying to protect the wolf. You've also got to protect what the wolf eats, including moose and deer. Moose and deer are both herbivores, so you have to make sure that the plants the moose and deer eat are thriving. In order for the plants to survive, it may be necessary to save the birds and insects that pollinate them.

Who saves habitat? Governments do, in parks and wilderness areas. Environmental groups do, too. For example, the Nature Conservancy, with the aid of contributions from members, buys land in order to keep it from being developed and the ecosystems destroyed. The Conservancy owns and manages more than 1,400 preserves, where people can see nature undisturbed.

Breed in Captivity. Zoos are no longer just for entertainment. Behind the exhibition areas in many zoos, scientists are working to help save species that are in trouble. For example, the Siberian tiger, largest of all the cats, is an endangered species, with only a few hundred left in the wild. Its natural habitat in southern and eastern Asia is shrinking.

But the species is doing very well in zoos. There are more than 700 Siberian tigers in about 230 zoos around the world. Only about 25 of these animals were caught in the wild and brought to zoos. The rest were born in captivity.

What good is a tiger in a zoo? Not much, according to some people. They believe that if a species can't survive in the wild, then people ought to let it become extinct with dignity. But most people, including those who watch over the captive tigers, hope to release tigers back into the wild someday. They're keeping the species alive in zoos until it's safe for them to go back to the wild.

Release to the Wild. Some animals (and plants, too) are in such bad shape that the only ones left alive live in zoos (or botanic gardens). The best thing that could happen to them would be to be bred in captivity and then released back to the wild. But a species can't be reintroduced into its native habitat if its native habitat no longer exists.

In a few cases, habitat has been protected or restored. Then, biologists may be able to return a species to the wild, if they can breed enough of the animals in captivity.

One of the first animals reintroduced was the Arabian oryx, a kind of antelope. Once fairly common in the deserts of the Middle East, it was decimated by hunters, who even used helicopters. The last wild oryx were shot in Oman in 1972.

Luckily, ten years earlier, some scientists saw the writing on the wall and brought several oryx to the Phoenix Zoo. They joined animals from other zoos to form a "world herd." By 1980, there were well over 100 captive oryx in the United States alone.

During 1980 and 1981, ten oryx were flown to Oman. They were released into a fenced-in area. The fence was put up so the animals could get used to the desert gradually. In early 1982, the fence was opened. Soon, an oryx was born—the first born in its natural habitat in 20 years. By 1996, the herd had grown to 400. But by 1999, poachers had reduced the number to 100. So the government of Oman put some of the wild oryx

back into enclosures for their protection. They are now working with other governments and environmental organizations to find a long-term solution for the oryx.

What You Can Do

• **Support your local zoo.** If it's a good one, that is, where the animals have room to roam and are healthy. Some small "roadside" zoos treat animals poorly; if you find one, write to elected officials asking to have it improved or closed.

• **Don't buy pets taken illegally from the wild.** When you go to a pet store to get tropical fish or birds, ask if the animals were bred in captivity or taken from the wild. You'll be showing pet store owners that you don't want wild-caught animals. Owners will provide what their customers want.

• **Don't buy a product if animals are killed to make it.** Ivory comes from dead elephants. Fur coats once kept an animal warm.

• **Cut apart the plastic six-pack holders your soda comes in before you throw them away.** Small animals can become entangled in these and other discarded packaging materials.

• **Educate others about the importance of habitat.** Encourage your friends and public officials to keep wild areas wild.

• **If your cat is a killer, handicap it.** Domestic cats kill birds and other wildlife. A bell around its neck gives its prey a chance to escape.

• **Write your congressman.** Let him or her know how important you think it is to maintain wilderness areas so wild animals have a home.

CONCLUSION: NOW WHAT?

Saving the planet is a team effort. Probably the most important step you can take is to learn more about the environment. Then you'll be in a position to change your own behavior, to influence your friends, and, most importantly, to influence decision makers. By knowing how government works, you and your friends can help bring about changes. That's how the kids in Freeport, Maine, got Styrofoam banned from their town. That's how the kids in Aurora, Colorado, and Milford, Connecticut, got tuna banished from school lunchrooms.

When you want your opinion heard, write your representatives in local, state, or national government. They will appreciate hearing from you.

Support environmental groups whose goals you share. These groups can often help you plan a project or direct you to experts.

Finally, be a "green consumer." Green is the color of the environment and green consumers keep the environment in mind when they shop. They buy recycled products. They avoid excess packaging. They boycott products that damage the environment or creatures in it.

The planet may be in trouble, but it's not too late to save it. The next few decades will be critical. It's your planet, so do something about it.

GLOSSARY

Acid rain: Rain and other precipitation that is more acidic than usual because of air pollution.

Agriculture: The growing of plants and the raising of animals in order to feed people.

Biological control: The use of biological methods, such as predators and parasites, to kill agricultural pests.

Carnivore: A meat-eating animal.

Climate: The average weather over a large area for many years.

Consumers: Species, usually animals, that eat producers or other consumers.

Decomposer: Species, such as bacteria and fungi, that eat the remains of dead plants and animals.

Ecology: The science that studies how living things interact with one another and with the physical environment.

Ecosystem: A physical place and the species that inhabit it.

Erosion: The gradual, or occasionally sudden, wearing away of soil or rock by wind and water.

Extinction: The death of an entire species.

Food web: The pattern of which species eat, or are eaten, by which other species.

Greenhouse effect: The gradual warming of the Earth's atmosphere because carbon dioxide and other gases prevent heat from escaping to space.

The **Green New Deal (GND):** Set of proposed economic stimulus programs in the United States that aim to address climate change and economic inequality.

Groundwater: Underground water, the source of wells and springs.

Habitat: The place where a species usually lives.

Herbivore: A plant-eating animal.

Mass extinction: The extinction of many species at the same time.

Nonpoint pollution: Pollution that. can't be traced to a single source but comes from many places. An example is the water pollution from pesticides that wash off fields.

pH scale: A scale from 0 to 14 that measures relative acidity. 0 is completely acidic, 7 is neutral, 14 is completely basic, or nonacidic.

Photosynthesis: A series of chemical reactions in which green plants use the Sun's energy to make food out of carbon dioxide and water, while releasing oxygen.

Predator: An animal that hunts and kills another animal for food.

Producer: Green plants, so named because during photosynthesis they "produce" food available to consumers.

Radioactive dating: A method of estimating the ages of rocks. The method works because radioactive elements in the rocks change into other elements at a constant rate.

Rain forest: Forests where the heavy rainfall leads to dense vegetation. Usually found near the equator, although there are cool rain forests as well, such as in southeast Alaska.

Species: A particular kind of plant or animal. The diamond-back rattlesnake is a species, as are the white-tailed deer and the sugar maple.

Topsoil: The top, fertile layer of soil.

Weather: The temperature, winds, and precipitation experienced in one place at one time.

ABOUT THE CONTRIBUTORS:

BILLY GOODMAN studied ecology at Princeton University and the University of Minnesota. He now writes about science and nature for adults and young Adults. He is a winner of a distinguished achievement Award for excellence in Educational Journalism and of an Excellence Award from the Society for Technical Communication. A former science writer at the American Museum of Natural History in New York City, Goodman lives in Brooklyn with his wife and two cats.

PAUL MEISEL was graduated from the Yale School of Art and worked as an art director before becoming a Full-time illustrator. He is a frequent contributor to the New York Times and illustrator of Mr. Bubble Gum, and Mr. Monster. Mr. Meisel lives with his wife and two children in Brookfield, Connecticut.

MAARTEN DE KADT, Ph.D., the consultant, is research associate at INFORM, an environmental research group.